THE COURAGE TO START

BREAKING FREE FROM FEAR AND PROCRASTINATION

LATTESSHA Y. JONES, PHD

THE MOTIVATION JOINT

CONTENTS

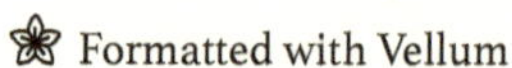 Formatted with Vellum

DEDICATION

To Boobie and Jay,
Every step I've taken, every mountain I've climbed, and every dream I've chased has been with you in mind. This book is a piece of my journey, but it's also a gift to you. Always remember: fear is just a feeling, not a stop sign. Walk in your truth, chase your dreams boldly, and never be afraid to start... even if your knees are shaking. You are my greatest inspiration. I hope this book reminds you of the strength, courage, and fire that lives within you.

INTRODUCTION: I WAS TERRIFIED

I know what it feels like to be scared out of your mind when it comes to chasing a dream. That dream sits heavy on your heart, plays on repeat in your head, and shows up every time you see someone else doing the very thing you wish you had the courage to do. You think about it in the shower, while you're driving, right before you fall asleep... but when it's time to actually do it? Fear and procrastination come knocking—loud.

"What will people say?"

"What if I fail?"

"What if I embarrass myself?"

"What if it doesn't work?"

Yeah, I've asked myself every one of those questions too. And yep, I almost let them stop me.

But here's the truth: fear doesn't disappear just because you've got a good idea. In fact, the bigger your dream, the louder fear gets. And procrastination? Whew, baby—procrastination is fear's sneaky little sidekick. It'll tell you things like, "Now's not the right time. Maybe next month. Maybe when you've got more money. Maybe when you're more prepared." It sounds logical, but it's really just fear in disguise. I know… because I lived it.

When I started writing, I was terrified. When I thought about starting a business, the what-ifs came storming in. When I decided to go back to school to pursue my doctorate, I questioned whether I was good enough or smart enough. When I wanted to step into the spotlight and use my voice, I thought, *Who's even going to listen to me?* Every single move I made toward the life I actually wanted came with doubt, insecurity, and the urge to run back to my comfort zone.

But here's the part I need you to catch…
I did it anyway.

I started scared. I stumbled. I second-guessed myself. I faced opposition—and yes, I even failed a few times. But each time I pushed past fear, I discovered something incredible. On the other side of fear was proof I was capable, and proof I was stronger than I thought. If you've ever felt stuck between wanting more and being afraid to begin, I recognize that place.

That's why I wrote this book for you.

I know you've got something inside you—an idea, a dream, a vision that won't leave you alone. It reminds you of its presence throughout the day. And I also know fear has been whispering to you, telling you to wait, convincing you that you're not ready, and keeping you stuck in procrastination over the very thing that could change your life.

This book is your sign to stop waiting. It's your reminder that courage doesn't mean you're not afraid—it means you move anyway. You don't need to have every detail figured out. You don't need to be perfect. You just need the courage to start. And let me share something I wish I understood sooner: the first step doesn't have to be pretty; it just has to be taken.

So, if you're holding this book, reading these words, it means you're ready. You're ready to stop overthinking, stop doubting, and stop letting fear and procrastination run your life. You're ready to start. And I'll be right here—walking with you through every chapter, telling you the truth, sharing my story, and pushing you forward when fear tries to pull you back.

Let's do this together.

BEFORE WE BEGIN
UNDERSTANDING THE JOURNEY

What Is Fear?

According to Webster, "fear is an unpleasant emotion caused by the belief that someone or something is dangerous, likely to cause pain, or a threat." Nice and tidy definition, right? But honey, Webster clearly never tried to launch a business or use the TikTok for the first time. (Yes, I said *the* TikTok—my kids are gonna have a fit when they read this). Still, fear runs deeper than a social media post. Some of it has been living in us for years—passed down through experiences, expectations, and even survival.

Dr. Na'im Akbar, a pioneer in African-centered psychology and author of *Breaking the Chains of Psychological Slavery*, explains that many of the mental barriers we carry are not formed in isolation. They are inherited beliefs—shaped by experience, culture, and conditioning—and often passed down through generations as a result of history, environment, and survival. He refers to this as *psychological bondage*: invisible chains that limit how we see ourselves and keep us locked in patterns of self-doubt and hesitation.

For me, this played out in a very real way, and I learned that fear doesn't always show up loud or dramatic. Most of the time, it sounds reasonable. It shows up as that quiet voice that says, *Play it safe,* or

You're not ready yet. It disguises itself as logic, when in truth, it's protection gone too far. Fear convinces you that standing still keeps you safe—but what it really keeps you is stuck.

Fear says, "Don't try. It might go wrong."

Courage says, "Try anyway. It might go right."

Fear's job is to warn you.

Your job is to move anyway.

What Is Procrastination?

Procrastination is fear wearing a disguise. It's not laziness—it's avoidance. Drawing from Dr. Na'im Akbar's teachings on psychological bondage, delay is often less about motivation and more about internalized beliefs that restrict action. These invisible chains sound like, "You're not ready," "You're not qualified," or "You'll fail anyway."

Experience has taught me this lesson—repeatedly. When you put something off, it's rarely the task you're avoiding, it's the feeling behind it. Fear of failure, fear of judgment, fear of success, and what it might demand from you. Every time you delay your purpose, you give fear more power. You teach your mind that fear gets the final say.

This book is about taking that power back. It's about breaking those chains and teaching your mind something new—that you're capable, that you're ready, and that courage doesn't wait for perfect timing.

What Does Courage Really Mean?

Courage isn't polished or pretty. It's messy movement in the right direction. Ain't nothing cute about it. For me, it was downright slobbery and ugly. But at the end of the day, it was still movement—taking action while my hands were shaking and my heart was racing. I learned that courage isn't just a feeling; it's a mindset. It doesn't show up out of nowhere—it's connected to how we think and feel.

Dr. Rheeda Walker, a clinical psychologist and author of *The Unapologetic Guide to Black Mental Health*, emphasizes that psychological fortitude is developed through emotional awareness and the willingness to face fear rather than avoid it. In my experience, operating in that willingness is where strength develops, and courage becomes action.

Taking that first step and moving forward with awareness and purpose doesn't mean that fear is absent it means you've decided to move through it. Courage means choosing truth over comfort. It means trusting yourself when doubt is standing in front of you, screaming in your face. It's realizing that everything you need is already inside you—you just have to grab it and use it.

That's what this whole journey is about: reconnecting with your inner power so you can stop waiting, stop apologizing, and start doing.

This is your starting line.

From here on out, I want you to show up for yourself with honesty, grace, and just enough boldness to move—even when it's uncomfortable. You don't have to have it all figured out.

You just have to begin.

THE COURAGE DECLARATION

I, _______________________, make this declaration today to show up fully for my own growth. As I move through this book, I commit to facing my fears, telling myself the truth, and doing the work with an open heart. I promise to be honest, patient, and brave even when it's uncomfortable. I understand that courage isn't about having no fear; it's about choosing to keep going anyway. This is my promise to lean in, to do the work, and stay open to whatever growth is waiting for me on the other side.

Signed: _______________________

1

THE VOICE IN YOUR HEAD

You ever notice how loud your thoughts get when you're about to do something that actually matters? I mean, the second you decide, *"Okay, I'm gonna start this business... I'm gonna launch this page... I'm going back to school... I'm writing that book,"* here comes that voice. And it doesn't whisper. Oh no—it shouts:

"What will people say?"
"What if they laugh?"
"What if nobody supports you?"
"What if you fail and everybody sees it?"

Sound familiar?

We all have that voice in our heads—the critic, the doubter, the second-guesser. And it's not just any voice. It's **your** voice. It sounds like you, with all your isms and quirks mixed in. It thinks like you. And it pretends it's protecting you.

Psychologists call this inner chatter *automatic thoughts*—those instant reactions your brain throws out when you're about to step into something new. Drawing from Dr. Na'im Akbar's work, fear doesn't always come from what's around us; sometimes it's rooted in the limits we've learned to place inside ourselves. But here's the thing: those thoughts aren't facts. They're just your brain's first reaction to fear. So, let's call it what it is... fear dressed up as logic.

THE LIE OF THE INNER CRITIC

That voice in your head will always lean toward the negative, because it's wired to keep you safe. Safe from risk. Safe from failure. Safe from embarrassment. But let me tell you the problem with safe. Safe is where dreams go to die.

If I had listened to that voice, I wouldn't have written a word. I wouldn't have gone back to school. I wouldn't have started anything. That voice told me, "You don't have time. You don't have the money. You don't have the support." And for a while? I believed it. It had me shook.

I procrastinated. I put things off. I kept telling myself, *"I'll do it later."* But later turned into weeks, and weeks turned into months. And finally one day, I looked in the mirror and thought, *"If I don't do something, I'll still be in the same spot five years from now."* That's when I knew I had reached my limit. I was tired of being stagnant, scared, and stuck. As my granny would say, *"I got sick and tired of being sick and tired."*

WHAT PEOPLE WILL SAY —AND WHY IT DOESN'T MATTER.

Let's tackle the number one fear head-on: *What will people say?* Honey, that one question will have you standing still and rob you of your momentum. The truth is, people will talk no matter what you do. If you chase your dreams, they're gonna talk. If you sit on the sidelines, they're still gonna talk. So why not let them talk while you're out here doing something that actually matters?

When I started putting myself out there, I heard it all. Some people thought I was "doing too much." Others thought I was "wasting my time." And a few just sat back, waiting to see if I'd fail. But their opinions didn't stop me from showing up. And as trifling as their words were, they didn't stop me from creating, from writing, and they definitely didn't stop me from living my life. And the more I think about it, the crazy thing is: the loudest critics are usually the quietest dreamers. They sit on the sidelines pointing fingers while you're out here in the game. And yes, they get big mad because your movement and progress remind them of everything they talked themselves out of.

This particular group of folks is also known as *haters*. Yep. I said it. And as my kids would say, "Ma, clock that tea." (They had to explain to me that this slang means to notice, observe, or recognize the truth about a situation.) So, don't ever give your power to someone who's too afraid to even show up for their own life.

Now... clock THAT tea.

MY STORY: WHEN THE VOICE OF DOUBT WAS LOUDEST

I remember when I first thought about writing a book. Whew, that voice was loud. It said, *"Guuuurl Stop! Nobody's going to read this. Who are you to write a book? You're not an author. Nobody's interested in what you have say."* And honestly? I almost believed it.

I sat on that dream for months. But it wouldn't let me go. It kept tapping on my spirit and tugging at my mind, whispering to me late at night, and following me throughout the day. Eventually, I realized something powerful: my dream was louder than my doubts. I just had to decide which voice I was going to believe.

So, I chose to write.

I was scared. Scratch that—I was terrified. Doubt didn't just whisper; it echoed, in my head, loud, relentless, and convincing. I was so unsure of myself that my hands were literally trembling over the keyboard. I froze, staring at them like, *Oh shit... Am I really doing this?* I pulled them back, curled them in against my chest, and gave myself a quiet pep talk. *You got this. You got this, gurl. You can do this. Let's do it.*

My heart was racing but I took a deep breath and started typing anyway. A few shaky words became a wobbly sentence. Then another. Then another. Some days, I stopped mid-thought, questioning whether I really wanted to keep going. Other days, I had to fight to stay focused—to quiet the noise in my head, to push past the fear, and keep typing.

And I did. I kept writing through the doubt, through the uncertainty, and through every moment that tried to convince me to stop. And when finally—Lawd, finally—I held that finished manuscript in my hands, after every delay, distraction, and night I almost quit, one truth was impossible to ignore: The voice of doubt had been lying all along.

SILENCING THE VOICE (PRACTICAL STEPS)

That little voice? Oh, it never fully leaves. But you *can* shut it down long enough to move. Here's how:

1. **Call it out.** The next time that voice says, *"What if you fail?"* respond with, *"What if I don't?"* Talking back to fear interrupts it and takes away its power.

2. **Write it down.** Grab a notebook and list the lies that voice is telling you. Then, next to each lie, write the truth. For example:
   - **Lie:** Nobody will care.
   - **Truth:** Somebody is waiting on this.

3. **Take a small step.** Don't wait for courage to come first. Do one thing scared. Post that video you've been working on. Write your first page. Complete that application. Do whatever it is that's true for you. Then watch fear shrink with every step you take.

4. **Limit the noise.** Protect your environment. Be mindful of who and what you allow into your space and your life. Limit your time with people who drain your energy. Feed yourself encouragement instead—positive words, music, and people who remind you who you are and what you're capable of.

THE TRUTH YOU NEED RIGHT NOW

Here's what I want you to hold on to: you'll waste your whole life waiting for approval that was never required. That voice in your head —the one that questions, hesitates, and negotiates—will always try to talk you out of your destiny. But at some point, you have to decide to move anyway.

You don't need permission.

You don't need a cheering section.

You don't need perfect conditions.

You just need to start.

The voice in your head is not the voice of truth. It's the voice of fear. And fear only has the power you give it.

YOUR TURN

I'm going to challenge you right here. Grab a notebook, open your notes app, or use the margins of this book to answer these questions honestly:

- What dream have you been putting off because you're afraid of what people will say?
- What's the loudest "what if" running through your head right now?
- And if fear wasn't a factor, what would you start today?

Write it down. Get it out of your head and onto paper. Take a good look at what you wrote. Seeing it on the page is the beginning of recognizing the truth for yourself—the only thing standing between you and your dream is that relentless little voice. And the moment you choose to move, that voice loses its power.

LET THIS SIT WITH YOU

Fear's voice will never shut up completely. But neither should yours. Every time you take a step toward your dream, you teach fear to quiet down. Every time you move, you prove that courage isn't about being fearless; it's about refusing to let fear win. And if nobody else has told you this today: You are capable. You are worthy. And you are ready.

"The voice in your head may be loud, but your dream deserves to be louder."

— DR. LATTESSHA JONES

2

THE WEIGHT OF 'WHAT IF'

I f fear had a favorite phrase, it would be *"what if."*

What if I fail?

What if it doesn't work?

What if people laugh?

What if I'm not good enough?

What if I waste my time, my money, my energy?

That little two-word question has stopped more dreams than failure ever has. Failure, at least, means you tried. *"What if"* means you never even got out the gate.

THE TRAP OF "WHAT IF" THINKING

Here's the problem with *"what if"*: it feels smart. It feels responsible. It feels like you're just "thinking it through." But most of the time, it's not planning—it's paralyzing.

"What if" will weigh you down like a backpack full of bricks. And the crazy part is, most of the things you're worried about never even happen. How many times have you stressed yourself out over something, only to realize later it wasn't that serious?

That's the power of *"what if"*. It makes the imagined scarier than the reality.

MY STORY: DROWNING IN "WHAT IF"

I remember when I first started thinking about going back to school for my doctorate. I hadn't taken a single step yet. It was just an idea. I hadn't decided on a school, filled out an application, nothing. All I knew was, I wanted to do it. But the very thought of taking on something that big had me stressed out. My mind was full of *what ifs*, and they made me feel stuck and defeated before I even had a chance to start.

"What if I don't get accepted into a doctoral program?"

"And if I do, what if I can't handle it?"

"What if I don't finish?"

"What if I can't keep up with the coursework?"

The way I was stressing, you'd think I'd already flunked out of the program I hadn't even applied to yet. I carried those what-ifs with me from the day I called the school to apply, to writing my admissions essay, getting accepted, and even registering for my first class. I almost talked myself out of showing up on the first day because I was scared out of my mind. And after exhausting myself with every worst-case scenario imaginable, I realized I needed a way to manage my fear—make it digestible enough to keep moving. So I flipped the script and started asking myself a new set of what-ifs.

"What if I get through this first class?"

"What if I actually succeed?"

"What if I graduate and this degree changes my future?"

"What if I inspire somebody else to keep going?"

And you know what? Those new *"what ifs"* felt lighter. They gave me energy instead of draining it. That's when I realized the *"what if"* game could be played both ways.

THE OTHER SIDE OF "WHAT IF"

Fear's "what if" always points to the negative. But courage's "what if" points to possibility.

Fear says, "What if you fall?"
Courage says, "What if you fly?"
Fear says, "What if nobody supports you?"
Courage says, "What if the right people show up when you need them most?"
Fear says, "What if you waste your time?"
Courage says, "What if this step changes your life?"

The "what ifs" are going to come either way. The question is: which ones will you believe?

PRACTICAL STEPS: FLIPPING YOUR "WHAT IFS"

Let's look at some ways to break free from the weight of *"what if"*:

1. **Catch it in real time.** The next time you hear yourself say "what if," pause. Write it down so you can see it.
2. **Flip it.** For every negative "what if," write down the opposite. (Example: "What if I fail?" → "What if I succeed?")
3. **Choose your focus.** You can't stop the negative "what ifs" from showing up, but you can choose which ones you focus on.
4. **Take one step anyway.** Don't wait for every "what if" to be resolved. Move forward and let real life answer the questions fear keeps asking.

THE TRUTH YOU NEED RIGHT NOW

"What if" can hold your dream hostage, or it can be the very thing that drives you forward. It all depends on how you use it. The difference between staying stuck and moving forward is which kind of "what if" you give your attention to. If you let fear's version win, you'll always play it safe. If you let courage's version win, you'll step into possibilities you never imagined.

YOUR TURN

Take a moment and be honest with yourself. Grab your notebook and do the following:

- Write down the top three "what ifs" that are holding you back right now.
- For each one, flip it into a positive "what if."
- Circle the positive versions and commit to focusing on those this week.

Example:

- *What if I fail? → What if I learn something that helps me succeed next time?*
- *What if nobody cares? → What if the one person who needs this sees it?*
- *What if I waste my time? → What if this is the step that opens the next door?*

LET THIS SIT WITH YOU

I know the weight of "what if" can feel heavy. I've carried it too. But let me remind you of something important: most of the things you're worried about will never happen. And even if they do, trust yourself. Trust your gifts. Trust your talents. Trust your ability to manage it and survive it. Don't let the fear of a possibility rob you of the reality of your potential. The next time "what if" shows up, answer it with courage.

"You'll never know the answer to "what if" until you actually do the thing."

— DR. LATTESSHA JONES

3

THE FEAR OF FAILURE

Most people talk about the fear of failure like it's the biggest thing stopping us. And don't get me wrong, it's huge. Nobody wants to fall flat on their face, waste time, or feel embarrassed. But here's something people don't talk about as much: sometimes the fear of success can be just as heavy.

Sounds crazy, right? But think about it. Failure feels scary because it feels like an ending. Success feels scary because it's a beginning. And both can make you freeze in place if you're not careful.

THE FEAR OF FAILURE: "WHAT IF I FALL?"

Failure gets a bad rap. We treat it like it's the enemy, like once you fail, it's over. But the truth is: failure is not final. It's feedback. Think about when you learned to ride a bike. Did you fall? Probably. Did you scrape your knees? Absolutely. Did you give up? Nope. You got back on. And eventually, you learned. That's what failure is. It's scraped knees and elbows. It hurts, but it doesn't end the journey.

When I first thought about writing a book, I was terrified of failing. I thought, *"What if nobody wants to read it? What if I put my heart out there and it's a flop?"* That fear nearly kept me from writing at all.

But then I asked myself a different question: *Is it better to fail by trying, or to fail by default because I never started at all?* That's when I realized that failure wasn't the thing I needed to fear. Regret was.

THE FEAR OF SUCCESS: "WHAT IF I ACTUALLY MAKE IT?"

Now let's flip it. Have you ever thought about what happens if you *do* succeed? Suddenly there's pressure. Expectations. Visibility. People watching, asking questions, maybe even depending on you.

I remember when I finally started putting myself out there and things actually worked. I thought I'd feel nothing but excitement, but instead I felt nervous. I was thinking *"Can I keep this up? What if I can't handle it? What if people start expecting too much?"* For me, the thought of success became just as intimidating as failure. Why? Because success meant change. It meant that if I actually pulled this off, I'd be stepping into something bigger than where I was then. And the thought of that unfamiliar path had me shaking in my slippers.

That realization helped me understand something important: sometimes, we don't fear failure at all. We fear outgrowing the version of ourselves we've gotten comfortable with. We fear the responsibility that comes with the success we've worked so hard for.

YOUR BRAIN IS ASKING, *"Can we really handle this next level? Can we really do this?"* And the answer is yes, you can. But you'll never know unless you step into it. So don't be afraid of the next level. Be afraid of staying stuck on the same one.

MY STORY: FAILURE AND SUCCESS IN REAL LIFE

When I finally decided to go back to school for my doctorate—when it was no longer just an idea in my head and I was ready to actually do the thing—I was excited, anxious, and terrified all at once. Terrified more than anything.

I had a full-time job, two kids who were active in every extracurricular activity under the sun, and a husband who, at the time, was an active-duty Army officer. And let me tell you, being a military officer's wife comes with its own extra set of responsibilities. Between the family, the job, the military functions, and the endless obligations, adding a doctoral program on top of it all felt... well, let's just say questionable.

Picture it: 2017. *(In my Sophia Petrillo voice—love me some Golden Girls, honey!)* My home office slash bedroom, in a little corner I carved out just for studying and classwork. Ya girl was nervous. It was the first day of my first class, and I was sitting in front of my laptop. I opened the syllabus, looked at the required readings and assignment expectations, and then slammed my laptop shut. It felt like too much. My brain was screaming, *"Gurrrrrrrl! What have you done?!"* And of course, all those *"what ifs"* came marching in. *What if I fail? What if I can't do this? What if I'm in over my head?*

But I took a deep breath, whispered a quick prayer, opened my laptop with wobbly hands, and started the first assignment anyway. And once I got going, I realized fear wasn't going to break me. It wasn't as impossible as it looked on paper. One paragraph turned into a page, one page turned into a submission, and before I knew it I was moving forward. When I stumbled, I learned, I adjusted, and I kept going. Taking it one day at a time, one class at a time, I eventually completed my coursework and moved on to writing my dissertation.

Now *that* was another episode of fear all by itself and I struggled through every part of it. My dissertation committee was about that life, and honey, they tested my gangsta. Every time I thought I had a solid draft, they kicked it back with what felt like hundreds of revisions. So, I rewrote, revised, resubmitted, got it kicked back, fixed what they wanted corrected, and sent it again—over and over.

There were moments I wanted to quit. Moments I questioned whether it was worth it—especially with all the stress, and not to mention the money it cost to keep going. It was mentally and physically exhausting. But I kept going, and eventually, after all that hard work, painful stumbling, and persistence, I successfully defended my dissertation and graduated.

And you'd think that was the end of the fear, right? Wrong. That's when the fear of success showed up. I wanted this for so long, and when it finally came, I almost sabotaged my next steps out of fear. Fear had me second-guessing whether I was ready to use my new credential, share my voice, and build something bigger—my motivational business.

I questioned whether I was capable, whether I was prepared, and whether I was enough. Then I remembered something important: I didn't need to have every step figured out. I just had to show up for the step I was on. The mindset that got me through school, one step at a time, is the same mindset that carries me forward.

PRACTICAL STEPS: BEATING BOTH SIDES OF FEAR

Here's how you fight back against both sides of fear:

1. **Redefine failure.** Stop calling it the end. Call it information. Call it practice. Call it a lesson.
2. **Expect success and prepare for it.** Ask yourself, *"What systems can I set up now to help me handle the next level?"*
3. **Visualize both outcomes.** What's the worst that can happen if you fail? You learn and try again. What's the best that can happen if you succeed? Your life changes. Either way, you win.
4. **Take the pressure off.** You don't have to carry the weight of the entire journey at once. Handle today's step. Tomorrow will bring its own strength.

THE TRUTH YOU NEED RIGHT NOW

Failure isn't the opposite of success; it's part of the route. Every person you admire has failed. Every person you admire has also felt the pressure that comes with success. The people you look up to didn't avoid fear or pressure. They learned how to move through it. And that same choice—to keep moving, even when it's uncomfortable—is available to you too.

YOUR TURN

Let's do some work right here:

- Write down one fear of failure that's been holding you back. (Example: *"If I start my business, I might lose money."*)
- Write down one fear of success that's been holding you back. (Example: *"If I succeed, I won't be able to handle the demand."*)
- For each one, write a truth statement that cancels it out. (Example: *"Even if I lose money, I'll gain experience."* or *"If demand grows, I'll learn to delegate."*)

LET THIS SIT WITH YOU

Fear of failure and fear of success are just two sides of the same coin. One says, *"Don't try—you'll lose."* The other says, *"Don't try—you can't handle winning."* Either way, fear's goal is the same: to keep you stuck. But you weren't made to stay stuck. You were made to grow, to stretch, to rise, to live the dream that keeps tugging at your heart.

So, here's my challenge: don't wait until the fear disappears. Move while it's still there. Fail forward. Succeed scared. Just move.

4

PROCRASTINATION: THE PRETTY LIE

Let's talk about procrastination, the sneakiest, smoothest liar of them all. Procrastination doesn't show up loud and obvious. Oh no. It shows up looking responsible, reasonable, and logical. It says things like:

"Now's not the right time."
"You should wait until you're more prepared."
"Let's just think about it a little longer."

Sounds harmless, right? But here's the truth: procrastination is fear dressed up in nice clothes. It's the *pretty lie* that convinces you that waiting is wisdom, when really, waiting is wasting.

THE ILLUSION OF THE "RIGHT TIME"

We love to tell ourselves we're just waiting for the right time. But let me ask you this—when has the "right time" ever actually shown up? Life doesn't hand out perfect conditions. There will always be bills to pay, kids to raise, jobs to work, and people to deal with. If you're waiting for things to calm down before you move, you'll be waiting forever. The "right time" isn't a date on the calendar. It's the moment you decide to start. Period.

MY STORY: THE DELAY THAT COST ME

There were seasons in my life when procrastination had me in a chokehold and nearly robbed me of real opportunities. When I first thought about starting my book, I kept saying, *"I'll start next week... after things settle down."* Next week turned into next month. Next month turned into next year.

I kept pushing it off because I thought I needed more time, more knowledge, and more confidence. But the truth was, I didn't need more time—I needed more courage. All that waiting didn't change a thing. Waiting didn't make me smarter or braver. All it did was keep me stuck in the same place, spinning my wheels, overthinking, and second-guessing myself while life kept moving forward.

Procrastination isn't about needing more time. It's about fear hiding behind excuses. And the longer I let it run the show, the more opportunities slipped right through my fingers—chances to share my voice, inspire people who needed my message, and take real steps toward walking in my purpose. I watched moments that could have been breakthroughs quietly pass me by, all because I kept waiting for a perfect time that never came.

THE COMFORT ZONE IN DISGUISE

Procrastination is dangerous because it feels safe. It convinces you that you're protecting yourself from failure, when in reality, you're shutting the door on progress. Every time you procrastinate, you choose comfort over growth. And comfort may feel good in the moment, but it suffocates your potential in the long run. Procrastination doesn't keep you safe; it keeps you stuck.

PRACTICAL STEPS: BREAKING THE CYCLE

So how do you break free from procrastination? Let me share a few things that made a real difference for me, and I believe they can work for you too.

1. **Start small.** Don't wait to feel ready. Pick one small action and do it today.
2. **Set a deadline.** Open-ended goals will always get pushed back. Give yourself a date—and honor it.
3. **Use accountability.** Tell a trusted friend or mentor about your plan. Sometimes outside accountability is the push you need.
4. **Do it messy.** Stop waiting for perfect conditions. Done messy is better than not done at all.
5. **Ask yourself the hard question.** Every time you catch yourself delaying, ask: *"Am I waiting because I'm preparing —or because I'm scared?"*

THE TRUTH YOU NEED RIGHT NOW

Procrastination is the dream killer that smiles while it strangles you. Harsh? Maybe. But it's true. Procrastination looks friendly, but it's stealing your time, your energy, and your chance to create the life you want. Every day you wait is a day you can't get back.

YOUR TURN

Grab a notebook and respond to the following:

- What dream or goal have you been procrastinating on?
- Write down the excuses you've been telling yourself. (*"I don't have time." "I'll start when the kids are older." "I need more money."*)

- Now flip the script. Write down one small step you can take today. Yes—today. Not tomorrow. Not next week.

Example:

- **Dream:** Start a business
- **Excuse:** I don't have enough money
- **Small step:** Research business names or set up a free website

LET THIS SIT WITH YOU

Procrastination is a liar, but it's a comfortable one. That's why so many people never move, they believe the pretty lie that waiting is safer. But time isn't waiting for you. And neither is your dream. You don't need perfect timing, you don't need all the answers, you don't need everything lined up. You just need to take the first step and keep moving. Because in the end...

"The dream won't chase you; If you want it, you've got to move."

— DR. LATTESSHA JONES

5

PERFECTIONISM WILL
KEEP YOU STUCK

If fear has a twin, its name is perfectionism. Perfectionism convinces you that you're just "trying to get it right." But really? You're just stalling. You're not chasing excellence, you're hiding. And the sad truth is perfectionism doesn't move you forward, it keeps you stuck.

THE TRAP OF PERFECT

Perfectionism says:

"I'll start when I have more money."

"I'll launch once my plan is flawless."

"I'll post when my video looks professional."

But let's be real, if you wait for perfect conditions, you'll be waiting forever. Perfect doesn't exist. And chasing it will have you running in circles instead of running toward your dream. When you have a dream that is burning like fire in your bones; You don't need perfect, you need progress.

MY STORY: WAITING FOR PERFECT

By now, you know how terrified I was to start writing. I've already shared the fear, the shaking hands, and the doubt that tried to stop me before I ever typed a word. But fear didn't just show up as panic; it also showed up dressed as perfectionism. My first attempt at writing a book was a whole hot mess. I completely stalled out. I typed a sentence... backspaced. Typed another... deleted it. Typed a third... erased it again. And that cycle went on for what felt like hours, day after day.

Many times, I was locked in a staring contest with a blinking cursor on an empty page, caught in a loop of overthinking and second-guessing. I told myself I needed the perfect idea, the perfect outline, the perfect words—convincing myself that every attempt wasn't good enough. Days turned into weeks, and all that waiting, all that perfectionism, and yes, all that fear were draining the life out of my dream to become an author. Working through that cycle helped me realize I didn't need perfect. I just needed to start with what I had. And once I started, I had to finish.

So, I typed a few words. Those became my first paragraph. Then the next page. And slowly, one chapter after another, the words began to flow. It wasn't perfect. It was messy. And sometimes it was down-right ridiculous. But I kept going. And you know what? When that book was finally finished and published, not one person said it should've been more perfect. What they said was: This helped me. This encouraged me. This inspired me.

EXCELLENCE VS. PERFECTION

There is a big difference between excellence and perfection.

- **Excellence** means doing the best you can with what you have, where you are.
- **Perfection** means never feeling like what you do is enough.

Excellence moves you forward. Perfection keeps you paralyzed. Point blank. Period. When you aim for excellence, you release the need to control everything. You accept that mistakes will happen and you'll learn along the way. But when you aim for perfection, you never get started because you're too busy polishing an idea instead of testing it in real life. I know because I lived it.

Remember that blinking cursor and empty page I told you about? That was me stuck in perfection mode, convincing myself I wasn't ready. But the moment I shifted to excellence: choosing to write my truth, learn through the process, and keep moving, the words started coming. And eventually, that book wasn't just an idea anymore; it became a finished work—one I hope inspires others not because it's perfect, but because it's real.

PRACTICAL STEPS: BREAKING FREE FROM PERFECTIONISM

Here's how you stop letting perfectionism keep you stuck:

1. **Redefine success.** Success isn't perfect. Success is done. Success is movement.
2. **Set "imperfect deadlines."** Give yourself a finish date—no matter what. Don't allow endless editing, tweaking, or planning to keep you stalled.
3. **Start ugly.** That first post, that first video, that first draft —it's allowed to be messy. The goal isn't perfect; it's progress.
4. **Remember the bigger picture.** The person who needs what you're creating doesn't care if it's flawless. They care that it exists and is available to them.

THE TRUTH YOU NEED RIGHT NOW

Perfect is the enemy of done. And done beats perfect every time. If you keep waiting for perfect, your dream will never see the light of day. But if you move forward, even with shaky steps, you'll get further than you ever imagined.

YOUR TURN

Time for a little exercise:

- Write down one thing you've been delaying because it's "not perfect yet."
- Circle the part of it that really matters. (Example: For a video, it's the message, not the background. For a book, it's the words, not the font.)
- Commit to taking one imperfect step this week. Post the draft. Record the video. Share the idea. Start messy.

LET THIS SIT WITH YOU

Perfectionism will keep you polishing a dream that never launches. It'll keep you stuck in a cycle of waiting, fixing, and doubting. But your dream doesn't need perfect; it needs you. Your voice. Your action. Your presence. So, stop waiting for perfect conditions. Stop trying to impress everybody with flawless execution. Start now, start messy, start scared; but just start. Because in the end...

"The world doesn't need your perfect. The world needs your try."

— DR. LATTESSHA JONES

6

WHEN PEOPLE DON'T GET IT
AND DON'T SUPPORT YOU

One of the hardest parts of chasing a dream isn't always the work itself. Sometimes, it's the reaction you get from people. When you finally build up the courage to say, "I'm going back to school. I'm starting this business. I'm launching this page. I'm writing this book," you hope for encouragement, positivity, maybe even a little excitement.

Instead... crickets

Or worse, comments like, "How many degrees do you need?" (Yes, a family member actually said that to me.) Or, "That's a waste of time." "Are you sure you can handle that?" "Don't you think you're too old to start now?" Even when they weren't saying it outright, people found ways to downplay my vision. When I told folks I was writing this book, I heard, "Who has time for that?" When I shared that I was going back to school for my doctorate, someone I thought was a friend said, "That's good, but I'm fine with my bachelor's." At first, I was frustrated. I wasn't looking for validation. I just wanted to share something important to me with the people I cared about. I remember thinking, *Well, excuse the hell out of me. First of all, I didn't ask you that. Second of all... really?*

Those reactions taught me an important lesson: sometimes you have to stop talking and make your move. Some people—even those who seem supportive—will intentionally try to derail your momentum. I learned to stop telling everybody my business, because the quickest way to crush a dream is to share it with the wrong people.

Protect your dreams. Not everyone will understand them. Not everyone will support them. And if you're not careful, the very people you go to for encouragement can snatch the wind right out of your sails.

THE STING OF OPPOSITION

Nothing cuts deeper than opening your heart to people you love and having them dismiss it. The closer they are, friends, family, the ones you thought would hype you up; the more it hurts when they don't. I had to learn not everyone is meant to understand your vision. Your dream was given to you, not them. And a lot of times, their doubt is not really about you at all. It's about them.

Your courage shines a light on their fear. Your movement reminds them of where they feel stuck. Instead of dealing with their own stuff, they project it back on you. That's why the comments sting. That's why the silence feels so heavy. It's not because your dream is too big. It's because your dream, and your pursuit of it, exposes the places in their lives where they gave up on their own dreams.

What I came to understand is the sting of their words won't break you if you let it fuel you. Every doubt, every side comment, every eye roll is proof that you are shaking something up. If your dream didn't matter, nobody would care. The opposition is confirmation that you are onto something worth fighting for. So yeah, it stings. But let it sting, then let it push you forward.

PRACTICAL STEPS: MOVING WITHOUT THEIR VALIDATION

Here's how you keep going even when people don't get it:

1. **Stop explaining.** You don't have to justify your dream to people who've already decided not to understand.
2. **Find your circle.** Look for people who do get it—mentors, friends, and communities who will support and encourage you.
3. **Set boundaries.** Limit how much you share with folks who bring doubt and negativity.
4. **Clap for yourself.** Celebrate your own wins, no matter how small. Don't wait for applause that may never come.

LET THIS SIT WITH YOU

Stop waiting for support and give yourself permission to start. The courage to move without the crowd is the very thing that will take you further than you ever imagined. Support feels good but it is not required. What matters most is that you move forward toward your purpose.

"Those who are meant to be part of your journey will find you along the way."

— DR. LATTESSHA JONES

7

DOING IT SCARED

Fear doesn't just disappear. You keep waiting for that magical day when you wake up with no nerves, no butterflies, no sweaty palms, and all the confidence in the world. News-flash: that day never comes. Confidence isn't what makes fear vanish. Finding a thread of courage to grab onto is what pulls you through it. Courage doesn't mean you're not scared. It means you move anyway. Doing it scared is that secret sauce. It's the key that unlocks everything you've been waiting for.

MY STORY: MOVING WHILE SHAKING

When I first started working toward my dreams, I thought fear would just disappear once I got going. Nope. Fear was still there, chillin' and riding shotgun. The only difference? I stopped letting it drive.

I can't tell you how many times I've done things with my knees knocking. I was terrified going back to school. I was scared when I started writing. I was downright nervous when I stood in front of people to speak. But I showed up anyway. My voice shook, but I spoke. My hands trembled, but I wrote. My stomach flipped, but I walked into the room anyway. And every single time I acted in spite of fear, the fear shrank. It didn't go away completely, but it lost its power. It wasn't the giant monster I imagined. Just smoke and shadows. The moment I moved, it started to fade.

Even today, fear still whispers. Sometimes it even tries to get bold. But now, confidence has grown louder with every step I've taken. I've learned that doing it scared is how dreams become reality. It's part of the journey, and you are totally capable of handling it.

PRACTICAL STEPS: HOW TO DO IT SCARED

So how do you actually do it scared? Here are some tools that helped me:

1. **Name the fear.** Say it out loud. (Example: "I'm afraid I'll look stupid.") Naming it takes away some of its power.
2. **Shrink the step.** Instead of thinking, "I have to do everything at once," break it down into one tiny move. Fear hates momentum.
3. **Talk back to fear.** Every time it says, "What if you fail?" answer, "What if I don't?"
4. **Anchor in your why.** When fear gets loud, remind yourself why you started. Your why has to be louder than your what-ifs.
5. **Move anyway.** Action is the only thing fear respects. The moment you move, fear starts losing ground.

THE TRUTH YOU NEED RIGHT NOW

Fear doesn't mean you're weak, it means you're human. And the fact that you're scared is proof that you're stepping into something that will grow you. Confidence isn't built in the waiting; it's built in the doing. Every shaky step forward plants a seed of boldness, and over time those seeds grow into confidence. You don't need to get rid of fear before you move, you need to decide that your purpose and your future are worth more than your fear.

YOUR TURN

Grab a notebook:

- Write down one thing you've been putting off because you're scared.
- Now ask yourself: "What's the smallest step I can take toward this today, even if I'm terrified?"
- Commit to taking that step within the next 24 hours. And when you do, remind yourself that you're not waiting for fear to leave; you're proving to yourself that you can move in spite of it.

LET THIS SIT WITH YOU

Courage makes fear lose its grip. Every time you choose to step forward, knocking knees and all, you prove that fear is not the driver of your life. So, take a deep breath and do it scared. You got this!

"FEAR MAY SHOW UP, but courage will show out."

— DR. LATTESSHA JONES

8

YOUR TURN TO MOVE

We've unpacked the fears. We've talked about the what ifs, the procrastination, the perfectionism, and the lack of support. You've read my stories. You've seen my truth laid bare. And by now, you know one thing for sure: fear doesn't just go away. It hangs around in the background, whispering its sweet nothings and trying to make you doubt yourself. But you can't let that stop you. You can't let fear's lies keep you stuck.

It's time to get your a** up—yep, I said it. Get your a** up. Shake it off. It's time to move forward. It's your turn to move. Not next month. Not next year. Not when things "calm down." The time is right now.

Listen. The timing will never feel perfect. The stars won't magically line up. Your dream is waiting on you to make the first move. You've done the reading. You've done the reflecting. You've done the wishing and the wondering. Now it's time for action. So, whatever your dream is, start it scared. Start it messy. Start it unsure—but start it. This chapter isn't about overthinking. It's about doing. Your future self is already clapping for you, saying, "Finally, you moved."

THE STANDSTILL THAT STEALS TIME

Staying stuck is easy. You tell yourself you're just "thinking it through" or "waiting for the right time," but deep down, you know what's really going on. Fear and procrastination are tag-teaming your dreams. You start convincing yourself you need one more sign, one more plan, one more perfect moment before you move. But the truth is, there will never be a perfect time.

Every minute you hesitate, time keeps moving. Opportunities keep passing. Doors that were once cracked open start to close. While you're second-guessing yourself, somebody out there who is less qualified and less prepared is stepping into the very space that was meant for you. Not because they're better, but because they moved.

If you don't move, nothing changes. You stay in the same place with the same excuses, wondering why life feels stuck on repeat. Fear will always whisper reasons to wait, but courage reminds you that waiting costs more than failing ever will. So stop letting your dreams collect dust while you convince yourself you're not ready. Start where you are. Use what you have. Trust that the moment you move, momentum will meet you. Your future self is waiting for you to believe that right now, you are enough, and everything you need to begin is already inside you.

MY STORY: THE FIRST STEP FORWARD

When I decided to write, it wasn't some dramatic leap. It was me sitting down, staring at a blank screen, and typing out a few shaky words. When I decided to go back to school, I didn't have the whole journey figured out. I didn't have a five-year plan or a fancy vision board. Now, don't get me wrong—I love a good vision board—but at that time, all I had was a dream and a decision to go for it. I started with one small move: filling out the application. And let me tell you something people don't always say out loud: those first steps are not cute. They're not polished. They're not Instagram or Tik Tok ready. They're messy, awkward, and downright sloppy sometimes. That's the part nobody really talks about. The part where you're unsure and second-guessing yourself every minute. The part where you're doing the work without feeling confident or prepared.

Most people show you the glow-up: the "I did it!" the degree in hand, the finished book, the success. They don't show you the late-night doubts, the nervous typing, the moments of pep talking yourself through it or — those *"Lord, what am I even doing?"* moments. They don't show the pile of snacks you swear were "fuel for creativity," or the ten-minute breaks that somehow turned into full Netflix episodes. But those hot-mess steps matter. Those unsure moments count. Big results don't start with confidence or perfection. They start with one small, messy step you choose to take anyway. And if you're waiting until you feel ready, polished, or perfect, you'll be waiting forever. Start messy. Move scared. Take the step. Because that's where transformation begins.

PRACTICAL STEPS: HOW TO MOVE FORWARD

Here's how you stop thinking and start moving:

1. **Pick one thing.** What's the dream? Writing, posting, applying, creating? Name it. Get clear about the one thing that has been sitting with you.
2. **Do the smallest step.** Don't overthink it. Write one page. Hit the record button. Fill out the form. Send the email. Whatever it is, just move.
3. **Set a timer.** Give yourself 20 minutes. Fear loses power when you give yourself permission to start.
4. **Don't evaluate too soon.** Stop worrying about whether it's good enough. First moves aren't meant to be perfect. They're meant to get you unstuck.
5. **Keep stacking steps.** Consistency is louder than fear. Keep showing up, one small move at a time.

THE TRUTH YOU NEED RIGHT NOW

You don't need a leap. You just need a step. And then another. And then another. It's not about doing it all today. It's about refusing to stay still. Every small move adds up. Every tiny act of courage gets you closer.

YOUR TURN

I'm going to challenge you right here. Look back at everything you've already survived, every time you moved scared and did it anyway. What did it teach you? Write down one truth you'll carry with you the next time fear tries to stop you. Remind yourself you've moved before, and you can move again.

LET THIS SIT WITH YOU

The move doesn't have to be huge. It doesn't have to be perfect. It just has to be yours. Start small. Start scared. Start shaky. But start.

"Fear doesn't win when you move".

— DR. LATTESSHA JONES

CONCLUSION: THE PUSH YOU NEEDED

If you've made it to this point, one thing is clear: you've got a dream that refuses to leave you alone. You've been carrying it, thinking about it, wrestling with it. And now, there's no more pretending you can just sit on it.

We've talked about fear. We've talked about that little voice that tells you you're not ready, not qualified, or not enough. We've talked about doubt, procrastination, perfectionism, lack of support, and all the things that make you hesitate. By now, you understand this truth: fear doesn't disappear. It just gets quieter when you move. And it only has power when you give it permission.

You already have proof that you can move scared. You've done it before. You can move unsure. You can move while your knees are shaking. So, the real question is; will you?

CONFIRMATION: YOU'RE READY

Hear me when I tell you — you don't need validation or permission from anybody. Not your family. Not your friends. Not your coworkers. Not the critics on the sidelines. Your dream is valid simply because it's yours. Your desire matters because it was placed in you for a reason. You are allowed to start. You are allowed to build. You are allowed to succeed. And for everybody who keeps saying, "I just need a sign... I just need confirmation," well, here it is. This book is your sign. This book is your confirmation. So go ahead and take it personal. You could've been reading any book right now, but you chose this one. That's not an accident. That's alignment. Something in you knows it's time to move, and I'm here tell you; you are ready.

Your future is bigger than your fear. On the other side of fear is freedom. On the other side of procrastination is progress. On the other side of doubt is discovery. Every step you take opens doors you didn't even know existed and builds confidence you didn't realize you had. Every single time you push past fear, you prove to yourself that the voice whispering "you can't" was lying all along. You've waited long enough. The life you keep picturing, the one that tugs at your spirit, is waiting on the other side of your next move. So, take that step. Move scared. Move unsure. Just move.

"You are capable. You are ready. Grab that thread of courage and start."

— DR. LATTESSHA JONES

ABOUT THE AUTHOR

Dr. Lattessha Jones is an author, life coach, motivational speaker, and U.S. military veteran who knows firsthand what it means to push through fear and keep moving forward. With a PhD in Health Services and a passion for helping others step into their purpose, she built *The Motivation Joint* to empower people to live boldly and set boundaries without apology.

Through her books, coaching, and motivational talks, Dr. Jones blends real-life grit with soul-deep encouragement, reminding people that courage isn't the absence of fear—it's the decision to move anyway.

Connect with her online at **www.MotivationJoint.com** and join the movement to live brave, bold, and unshakably you.